Traveling in
TENNESSEE

Jim O'Rear

Schiffer Publishing Ltd

4880 Lower Valley Road • Atglen, PA 19310

Other Schiffer Books by the Author:
Tennessee Ghosts   ISBN 978-0-7643-3118-3 $14.99
Hollywood Paranormal Films: Fact & Fiction   ISBN 978-0-7643-3812-0 $19.99

Copyright © 2012 by Jim O'Rear

Library of Congress Control Number: 2012945386

Designed by Justin Watkinson Cover by Bruce Waters
Type set in Occidental/Brisa/Book Antique/Zurich BT

ISBN: 978-0-7643-4137-3
Printed in China

Published by Schiffer Publishing, Ltd.
4880 Lower Valley Road
Atglen, PA 19310
Phone: (610) 593-1777; Fax: (610) 593-2002
E-mail: Info@schifferbooks.com

For the largest selection of fine reference books on this and related subjects, please visit our website at **www.schifferbooks.com**.
You may also write for a free catalog.

This book may be purchased from the publisher.
Please try your bookstore first.

We are always looking for people to write books on new and related subjects.
If you have an idea for a book, please contact us at proposals@schifferbooks.com

Schiffer Books are available at special discounts for bulk purchases for sales promotions or premiums. Special editions, including personalized covers, corporate imprints, and excerpts can be created in large quantities for special needs. For more information contact the publisher.

In Europe, Schiffer books are distributed by
Bushwood Books
6 Marksbury Ave.
Kew Gardens
Surrey TW9 4JF England
Phone: 44 (0) 20 8392 8585; Fax: 44 (0) 20 8392 9876
E-mail: info@bushwoodbooks.co.uk
Website: www.bushwoodbooks.co.uk

To Lisa and Brandon,
who travel with me in my heart
when I'm on the road alone.

Special thanks goes to the managers/owners of the locations covered in this book, for their time and generosity in allowing me to spend all of the time needed on their properties to put together information and photos for use on these pages.

"To travel is to possess the world."

-Burton Holmes

Contents

Preface

As an entertainer, I have had the opportunity to travel from coast to coast and experience various cultures, see historical sites with my own eyes, witness the day-to-day lifestyles of the area locals, and take part in some significant events. In all of these various travels, though, Tennessee remains fascinating to me and I am always pleasantly surprised by new wonders that I encounter every time I travel through the state.

I'm a very visual person. Images tend to move me and speak to me much more than words. In creating this book, I set out to capture a variety of images that visually made a statement about Tennessee, from some of the more well-known tourist attractions to many of the lesser-known and unseen areas of the state. I wanted to let the reader visually experience the culture, lifestyle, history, religions, and people that

Elizabethtown, Tennessee.

Farm Life. Franklin, Tennessee.

Tennessee...home of Elvis Presley's Graceland, the great Smoky Mountains, the Chattanooga Choo Choo, Beale Street, the Country Music Hall Of Fame, Civil War battlefields, Music City, the Grand Ole Opry, and so much more. Tennessee is one of those rare states that is steeped in history and comfortably mixes quiet country living with bustling industry.

Gatlinburg, Tennessee.

The Chattanooga Star. Chattanooga, Tennessee.

The General Jackson. Nashville, Tennessee.

Country music star Mandy Barnett in South Pittsburg, Tennessee.

Brandon O'Rear in Cookeville, Tennessee.

make up Tennessee. I didn't want to bog down the reader with a lot of descriptive words. Instead, I wanted the images to speak for themselves and hopefully fill the viewer of those images with the same emotions and feelings that I experienced when I first came upon the locations.

This book is, by no means, a comprehensive guide to Tennessee or an attraction-to-attraction handbook — nor is it meant to be. It is a visual celebration of the state and the people who live there.

I hope you enjoy this exciting trip through the state of Tennessee.

Thanks for reading!
– Jim O'Rear

Sunset in Elizabethtown, Tennessee.

Ted Alderman practices in the fields.

No Chickens!

Chapter 1
A Brief History

The first people to live in the area we now know as Tennessee were the prehistoric Mound Builders. Then, several Indian tribes hunted in and claimed portions of the area now constituting Tennessee. Chief among these tribes were the Shawnee, who abandoned the area before the Europeans arrived; the Chickasaw, who claimed the western part, but did not live there; the Creek, who hunted in the midsection; and the Cherokee, who claimed the central and eastern areas, but only lived east of the Holston and Tennessee rivers, mainly along and south of the Little Tennessee River.

Tennessee's name is taken from the Tennessee River, the name of which is derived from that of a Cherokee Indian village called Tanasie, meaning "crooked ears," or more simply," crooked river."

Tennessee River, Mississippi River, Cumberland River, Clinch River, and Duck River.

The Tennessee area was explored by the Spanish in the mid-sixteenth century and by the English and French in the late seventeenth century. Hunters began crossing the mountains from the British colonies on the Atlantic coast in the 1760s and they were soon followed by permanent settlers. By the 1770s, many families had settled from Virginia and North Carolina.

A watchtower rests in the Cumberland River.

North Carolina gained control over the region in 1788 and then ceded it to the United States government, which organized it as the Southwest Territory in 1790.

By 1795, the population was 70,000. A petition was given to Congress to change Tennessee from a territory to a state, sparking a lively debate between the Jeffersonian Democratic-Republicans and the Federalists. While the Federalists were opposed to giving Tennessee statehood, the Jeffersonian Democratic-Republicans were successful and President George Washington signed a bill, on June 1, 1796, that gave statehood to Tennessee, the sixteenth state of the Union.

"In Tennessee, where I grew up, there were animals, farms, wagons, and mules."
— Tina Turner

Current residents of Tennessee have their choice of lifestyles, jobs, and living arrangements. With homes varying from quiet cabins in the woods to high-rise industrial buildings, and an assortment of jobs ranging from farmhand to music industry mogul, Tennesseans are not limited in their options.

Quite, country living in South Pittsburg, Tennessee.

Several traditional houses still stand throughout Tennessee.

Upscale living in Franklin, Tennessee.

13

Cost of living

9% lower than the national average

Housing

20% lower than the national average

Healthcare

9.7% lower than the national average

The climate is moderate, with four distinct seasons:

Average annual temperature:
58° F

Average high temperature:
January: 49° F
July: 86° F

Average low temperature:
January: 28° F
July: 69° F

An unfortunate architectural gem of the past.

A mansion on a hill in Gatlinburg, Tennessee.

Eerie Von, of Danzig, takes a break.

Tennesseans hold on to their traditions...and their classic cars.

Upscale country living just outside of Nashville, Tennessee.

Farming plays a large part in the Tennessee lifestyle. The climate is great for crop growth and the state receives approximately 50 inches of rain each year, with nursery products, soybeans, and corn making up the top crops. Tennessee has 27 million acres of land and 10.9 million acres of it is used as farmland. Additional land is used for forestry, bringing the total to 80 percent of the state being used for agricultural purposes.

Tennessee Humor

You know you're from Tennessee when you describe the first cool snap (below 70 degrees) as good pinto-bean weather.

Top 5 Agriculture Commodities

Type	Value of Receipts Thousand $	Percent of State Total Farm Receipts	Percent of US Value
Soybeans	564,593	19.9	1.9
Broilers	442,148	15.6	2.0
Cattle and Calves	423,767	14.9	1.0
Greenhouse/ Nursery	291,689	10.3	1.8
Corn	251,209	8.8	0.6

There are 2,040,000 cattle, 131,400 goats, 2,808,000 chickens, and 210,000 horses in Tennessee, with dairy cattle producing over 909 million pounds of milk each year and chickens producing 323 million eggs per year. The state also ranks #2 in the United States for hardwood and #3 for tobacco production.

Jim Hardin's southern lifestyle.

18

The Tennessee state motto is taken from wording featured on the 1801 great seal of Tennessee. The motto is symbolically represented on the seal by a picture of a plough, a sheaf, and cotton stalk, which all contribute to represent the state values attributed to agriculture. Commerce is symbolized by a picture of a riverboat.

On the eve of the Civil War, only one percent of Tennessee's population was employed in manufacturing, mostly in the iron, cotton, lumber, and flour-milling industries. Rapid industrial growth took place during the twentieth century, however; by 1981, Tennessee ranked third among the southeastern states and fifteenth in the United States in value of shipments. Tennessee's four major metropolitan areas – Memphis, Nashville, Knoxville, and Chattanooga – employ about half of all the state's industrial workers.

From 1987 to 1992, fifty-four industrial and commercial machinery manufacturers announced new plant locations in Tennessee while 366 existing companies in the industry expanded plant facilities. The state ranks fourth, nationally, in auto production. The seven largest industries in the state of Tennessee, next to farming, are mining (coal), electrical power, enriched uranium production, music, automobile manufacturing, walking horses, and tourism.

Industry at work in Nashville, Tennessee.

You know you're from Tennessee if you can name all four seasons: Almost Summer, Summer, Still Summer, and Christmas.

This type of housing is common in Gatlinburg, Tennessee, in order to look over the Smoky Mountains.

Railways have almost become a thing of the past in Tennessee.

AN Y JAIL WORKS

Too much peyote!

Population

Year	Rural	Urban	Total
1980	1,316,474	3,274,549	4,591,023
1990	1,348,082	3,529,103	4,877,185
2000	1,566,995	4,122,288	5,689,283
2010	1,686,343	4,659,762	6,346,105

Country music star Mandy Barnett.

Mansion living in Pigeon Forge, Tennessee.

Halloween haunts. Mt. Juliet, Tennessee.

Christmas time in Nashville, Tennessee.

Classic, Civil War era housing in Lebanon, Tennessee.

Skyline. Nashville, Tennessee.

Chapter 3

Music City U.S.A.

"There's nothing like Nashville for making records."
— Carol Channing

Nashville is the capital of Tennessee and the county seat of Davidson County. It is located on the Cumberland River, in the north-central part of the state. The city is a center for the health care, publishing, banking, and transportation industries and is home to a large number of colleges and universities. It is most notably known as a center of the music industry, earning it the nickname of "Music City U.S.A."

Nashville was founded by James Robertson, John Donelson, and a party of Wataugans in 1779, and was originally called Fort Nashborough, after the American Revolutionary War hero Francis Nash. Nashville quickly grew because of its strategic location, accessibility as a river port, and its later status as a major railroad center.

The "Batman Building." Nashville, Tennessee.

Nashville Fun Fact

The first-ever combination candy bar was invented in Nashville at the Standard Candy Company in 1912 by Mr. Howard Campbell. This famous Nashville candy made of chocolate, caramel, marshmallows, and peanuts is called a "GooGoo Cluster."

The Customs House. Nashville, Tennessee.

WKDF radio. Nashville, Tennessee.

Skyline. Nashville, Tennessee.

LP Field. Nashville, Tennessee.

In 1997, Nashville was awarded an NHL expansion team, which was subsequently named the Nashville Predators. LP Field (formerly Adelphia Coliseum) was built after the NFL's Houston Oilers agreed to move to the city in 1995. The NFL team debuted in Nashville in 1998 at Vanderbilt Stadium and LP Field opened in the summer of 1999. The Oilers changed their name to the Tennessee Titans.

The downtown area of Nashville features a diverse assortment of entertainment, dining, cultural, and architectural attractions. The Broadway and 2nd Avenue areas feature entertainment venues, night clubs, and an assortment of restaurants. North of Broadway lies Nashville's central business district, Legislative Plaza, Capitol Hill, and the Tennessee Bicentennial Mall. Cultural and architectural attractions can be found throughout the city.

Nashville's other sporting event arena, the Bridgestone Arena.

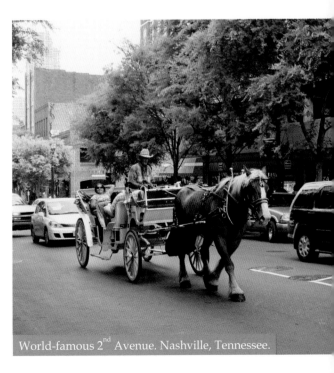

World-famous 2nd Avenue. Nashville, Tennessee.

Broadway nightlife. Nashville, Tennessee.

There are always street performers to be found in Nashville.

The Tennessee State Capitol building is quite a sight to behold. Located on the highest summit in the city, it is one of the most highly regarded Greek Revival style buildings in the nation. Built in the mid 1840s and costing $879,981.48, it was one of the most magnificent public buildings of its time anywhere in the United States, with pieces of it designed to match the monument of Lysicrates in Athens, Greece. The interior design was elegant as well, due to the extensive and masterful use of cast iron, an avant-garde building material in the 1840s.

Statue of Andrew Jackson, Tennessee Capitol Building.

33

Tennessee Capitol Building ...

Horror movie actress Debbie Rochon outside the Tennessee Capitol Building.

34

The U.S. Army Corps of Engineers maintains parks on Old Hickory Lake and Percy Priest Lake. These parks are used for multiple activities, including fishing, water-skiing, sailing, and boating. Percy Priest Lake is also home to the Vanderbilt Sailing Club.

Nashville Fun Fact

The first guide dog for the blind in the United States lived in Nashville with her owner, Morris Frank. "Buddy" was trained in Switzerland by The Seeing Eye, the first organization to train guide dogs.

The next location I'm going to mention may sound like an odd entry because it is a hotel. However, this hotel has become a major tourist attraction in the Nashville area due to the wide range of activities that take place there, as well as the architecture of the building itself. That hotel is the Gaylord Opryland Resort and Convention Center.

The Gaylord Opryland Resort and Convention Center, formerly known as Opryland Hotel, is the largest non-casino hotel in the Continental United States outside of Las Vegas.

The property, given a general theme toward "southern hospitality," opened as The Opryland Hotel in 1977, adjacent to the Opryland U.S.A. theme park and the Grand Ole Opry house, from which the hotel took its name. The hotel originally featured 600 guest rooms, a 20,000-square-foot ballroom, and 30,000 square feet of convention space.

In 1983, six years after opening, Opryland Hotel completed its first major expansion, dubbed "Phase II." This large undertaking added 467 guest rooms, moving the total to 1,067. Phase II also brought 30,000 square feet more of ballroom space and added the hotel's first signature atrium, the Garden Conservatory. Under large panes of glass and filled with plant life and fountains, the Garden Conservatory is designed to allow guests to experience a walk in a tropical garden without going outdoors. Hundreds of rooms have balconies overlooking the Conservatory. This was the first truly unique thing the hotel had to offer, and it set the stage for the next two expansions.

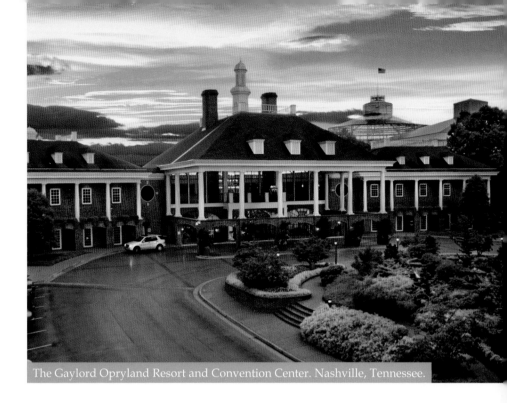
The Gaylord Opryland Resort and Convention Center. Nashville, Tennessee.

Inside the Opryland Hotel's Delta.

The Gaylord Convention Center.

By 1988, Opryland Hotel had expanded to 1,891 guest rooms. In the "Phase III" expansion, another 18,000-square-foot ballroom was added along with the Cascades, a second atrium designed to complement the Garden Conservatory. The Cascades is covered by an acre of glass and features thousands of plant species and large artificial waterfalls. As part of Phase III, but delayed by one year, another 4 ,000-square-foot ballroom opened, designed for more intimate settings and smaller functions.

Separate from the Phase III expansion was the addition of an 18-hole golf course, "Springhouse Golf Club," located two miles east of the hotel. The par-72 links-style course was home to the Bell South Senior Classic at Opryland on the Champions Tour from 1994 to 2003. It was renamed "Springhouse Links" in 2001, and then "Gaylord Springs" in 2006.

Opryland Hotel completed its "Phase IV" expansion in 1996. The $175-million "Delta" added 922 guest rooms, bringing the total to its current 2,881, and was the largest construction project in the history of Nashville at the time. (It was eclipsed in 1999 by Adelphia Coliseum, now known as LP Field.) Also part of the expansion, which more than doubled the size of the existing structure, was an additional 55,465-square-foot ballroom, a 289,000-square-foot exhibit hall, and the Delta Atrium. The 150-foot tall, 4.5 acre atrium was given a Cajun theme, borrowing many elements from New Orleans, Louisiana. Also under the large glass roof is the Delta River, a quarter-mile artificial waterway. For a $9 fee, guests may ride in a "Delta Flatboat" through a guided tour of the atrium. When it was christened, water samples from more than 1,700 rivers throughout the world, including every registered river in the United States, were poured into the Delta River.

Inside the Opryland Hotel's Delta.

While Gaylord Opryland caters largely to the out-of-town convention market, it serves a large purpose for the local community as well. Many local high schools use the ballroom space for their yearly proms. It is also known for being one of Nashville's hottest "first-date" spots because of its central location, restaurants, walkways, and scenery. Many local companies also take advantage of the Convention Center's abundant meeting space. Unlike most other non-casino hotels, a sizable portion of

Gaylord Opryland's visitors are not actually guests of the hotel. The scenery of the various atria along with the various shops and dining options attract many walk-in visitors to the hotel every day.

Tennessee Humor

"Onced" and "twiced" are words.

Statue of Tom Ryman.

The historic Ryman Auditorium.

As the city's name itself is a metonym for the country music industry, many popular tourist sites involve country music, including the Country Music Hall of Fame and Museum, Belcourt Theatre, and Ryman Auditorium. The Ryman was home to the Grand Ole Opry until 1974 when the show moved to the Grand Ole Opry House nine miles east of downtown. The Opry plays there several times a week, except for an annual winter run at the Ryman.

The building we know today as the Ryman was originally opened in 1892 as the Union Gospel Tabernacle. Captain Tom Ryman, a steamboat captain and hard-drinking hell raiser, found God after hearing an evangelist speak. He gave up his "evil" ways and began construction on a building that would be dedicated to religious revivals and activities. When Captain Tom died, in 1904, the tabernacle was renamed the Ryman Auditorium and soon became one of the most famous entertainment venues in the world.

The historic Ryman Auditorium ....

Inside The Ryman. ...

The Grand Ole Opry set to perform inside The Ryman.

The Ernest Tubb Record Shop. Nashville, Tennessee.

Another building near the Ryman with a huge connection to the country music industry is the Ernest Tubb Record Shop. Founded by legendary musician Ernest Tubb, the store has been providing country, gospel, and bluegrass music products to the public for almost sixty years. Tubbs is also the home base for the "Midnight Jamboree," America's second longest running radio show. The Jamboree airs on Saturday nights following the Grand Ole Opry and is host to a multitude of Opry stars.

Numerous music clubs and honky tonk bars can be found in downtown Nashville, especially the area encompassing Lower Broadway, Second Avenue, and Printer's Alley, which is often referred to as "The District."

Printers Alley. Nashville, Tennessee ...

One of the most famous honky tonks in the city is Tootsie's Orchid Lounge, located next to the Ryman. It is filled with memorabilia and always features some of the best musical acts in Nashville.

Originally called "Mom's," Tootsie Bess bought the bar in 1960 and, after it was mistakenly painted an orchid color, the name was changed to Tootsie's Orchid Lounge. Many of her first customers were Willie Nelson, Mel Tillis, Waylon Jennings, Kris Kristofferson, and Patsy Cline. In fact, Willie Nelson got his first song-writing job after singing at Tootsie's.

Tootsie's Orchid Lounge. Nashville, Tennessee.

Actor Bryan Wilson and author Jim O'Rear walk the red carpet during a Tootsie's event.

Tootsie loved music and helped these struggling artists whenever she could, often slipping money into their pockets and feeding them for free. She kept an IOU box stuck behind the counter so that the artists didn't feel as if they were "charity cases." Each year members of the Grand Ole Opry would pool money together and pay off all of the IOUs so that Tootsie would not lose any money.

Tootsie's Orchid Lounge. Nashville, Tennessee.

World-famous waitresses of Tootsie's.

Inside Tootsie's Orchid Lounge. Nashville, Tennessee.

Actor Bryan Wilson, country music legend Kris Kristofferson, and author Jim O'Rear backstage during an anniversary celebration for Tootsie's.

Nashville Fun Fact

President Theodore Roosevelt coined the phrase "good to the last drop," words that became a national slogan after sipping coffee at the Nashville Maxwell House Hotel. The coffee was a local product of the Cheek family. Their family home is now Cheekwood Botanical Garden and Museum of Art, located about eight miles southwest of downtown.

Country Music Television building. Nashville, Tennessee.

One-stop shopping for stringed instruments in Music City U.S.A.

Statue of Chet Atkins in downtown Nashville.

In 1964, sisters Margaret and Elise Croft donated property to the Children's Museum of Nashville. After the last sister's death in 1985, the Children's Museum began to develop about 40 of the property's 200 acres, which in 1990, became Grassmere Wildlife Park. Seven short years later, Grassmere Wildlife Park closed its doors because of low attendance and was given the option, by Mayor Phil Bredesen, to develop a zoo for Nashville on the property, exhibiting about 300 animals from around the globe.

Nashville Zoo inhabitants ...

Grassmere. Nashville, Tennessee.

There are many other historically important sites to see when traveling in the central Tennessee area, just outside of Nashville. One of those is the location of one of the most famous paranormal hauntings, ever…the only documented haunting where a ghost has actually killed a human being and the subject of numerous books, documentaries, and feature films. It is the incredible story of The Bell Witch, a spirit named "Kate" that haunted the Bell family, in the town of Adams, from 1817 to 1821.

Even today, over 150 years after she first appeared in Robertson County, "Kate" continues to hold some people in the town of Adams, Tennessee, in a state of intimidation.

Nashville's Belle Meade Plantation was famous for breeding thoroughbred horses. Iroquois, bred at the Belle Meade Farm, was the first American horse to win the English Derby. In addition to Iroquois, though, there were two other famous horses that can trace their lineage back to Belle Meade: Seabiscuit and War Admiral, both made popular again by the 2001 best-selling novel.

Inside the Bell Witch Cave. Adams, Tennessee.

Looking out of the Bell Witch Cave. Adams, Tennessee.

The former home of Tennessee icon and seventh American president Andrew Jackson is located just outside of Nashville and sits on an estate of 1,120 acres, which includes the entire 1,050-acre tract that Jackson owned when he died in 1845. Simply known as The Hermitage, the plantation was a place of refuge for the General. The building's architecture is a blend of Federal, Palladian, and Greek Revival styles. Today, it has been completely restored to the condition it was in during the years of 1837 through 1845, including most of the original furnishings that were recovered from family members and collectors. The former president loved the property so much that he had himself and his wife, Rachel, entombed in the Hermitage mansion garden.

The Hermitage...

Ministers are to be dedicated to God and therefore are not eligible to hold a seat in either House of the Legislature.

Andrew Jackson's tomb at The Hermitage.

The Parthenon.

The Parthenon in Nashville, Tennessee is a full-scale replica of the original Parthenon in Athens. It was built in 1897 as part of the Tennessee Centennial Exposition. Nashville's moniker, the "Athens of the South," influenced the choice of the building as the centerpiece of the 1897 fair. A number of buildings at the Exposition were based on ancient originals; however, the Parthenon was the only one that was an exact reproduction. It was also the only one that was preserved by the city.

Originally built of plaster, wood, and brick, the Parthenon was rebuilt on the same foundations, in concrete, in a project that started in 1920; the exterior was completed in 1925 and the interior in 1931.

Today, the Parthenon, which functions as an art museum, stands as the centerpiece of Centennial Park, a large public park just west of downtown Nashville. Alan LeQuire's 1990 re-creation of the Athena Parthenos statue is the focus of the Parthenon just as it was in Ancient Greece. The building is a full-scale replica of the Athenian original and the statue of Athena Parthenos within is a reconstruction of the long-lost original to careful scholarly standards: She is cuirassed and helmeted, carries a shield on her left arm and a small (six-foot) statue of Nike (Victory) in her right palm, and stands forty-two feet high, gilt with more than eight pounds of gold leaf. An equally colossal serpent rears its head between her and her shield. Since the building is complete and its decorations were polychromed as close to the presumed original as possible, this replica of the original Parthenon in Athens serves as a monument to what is considered the pinnacle of classical architecture.

Cheekwood.

Cheekwood.

Cheekwood is a privately funded 55-acre estate on the western edge of Nashville that houses the Cheekwood Botanical Garden and Museum of Art. Formerly the residence of Nashville's Cheek family, the 30,000-square-foot Georgian-style mansion was opened as a museum in 1960.

Cheekwood's art collection was founded in 1959 upon the holdings of the former Nashville Museum of Art and is accredited by the American Association of Museums. The core holdings include broad collections of American art, American and British decorative arts, and contemporary art, especially outdoor sculpture acquired for the Woodland Sculpture Trail. Extending across the grounds from the Museum of Art, the Botanical Garden encompasses the entire fifty-five-acre site with an emphasis on display, education, and study. The plant collections include boxwood, conifer, crape myrtle, daffodil, daylily, dogwood, fern, herb, holly, hosta, hydrangea, Japanese maple, magnolia, redbud, and trillium.

Cheekwood.

Cheekwood Botanical Gardens ...

Just south of Nashville rests the small town of Lynchburg, best known as the location of the Jack Daniel's distillery, whose famous whiskey is marketed world-wide as the product of a city with only one traffic light. Strangely enough, despite the operational distillery, Lynchburg's home county of Moore is a dry county. Lynchburg was also the home of Davy Crockett and is the current home of classic rock-and-roll artist Little Richard.

Jack Daniel's Distillery. Lynchburg, Tennessee.

Statue of Jack Daniel.

Jack Daniel's firehouse.

Jack Daniel's Distillery. Lynchburg, Tennessee ...

Jack Daniel's is a brand of sour mash Tennessee whiskey that is among the world's best-selling liquors. It is known for its square bottles and black label. As of November, 2007, it was reportedly the best-selling whiskey in the world and is produced by the Jack Daniel Distillery, which has been owned by the Brown-Forman Corporation since 1956. Although the product generally meets the regulatory criteria for classification as a straight bourbon, the company disavows this classification and markets it simply as "Tennessee whiskey" rather than "Tennessee bourbon."

Jack Daniel founded the distillery in 1866, although there seems to be some discrepancy in this date that can't be rectified due to records being destroyed in a courthouse fire. He took his nephew, Lem Motlow, under his wing and gave him the distillery in 1907 when Jack's health began to fail.

Tennessee passed a state-wide prohibition law in 1910, preventing the legal distillation of Jack Daniel's in the state and, as a result, Lem Motlow moved the distillery to St. Louis, Missouri, and Birmingham, Alabama, though none of the production from these locations was ever sold due to quality problems. All production then ceased. Even the Twenty-first Amendment enactment in 1933 repealing federal prohibition did not allow production in Lynchburg to restart, as the Tennessee state prohibition laws were still in effect. Motlow, as a Tennessee state senator, helped repeal these laws, allowing production to restart in 1938. Now, the distillery is visited by a multitude of tourists each year who go to see this unique and important piece of Tennessee history.

Nashville skyline during the 4th of July celebrations.

The sites around the surrounding Nashville areas do not stop there. One could fill volumes on this city alone. Today, the city along the Cumberland River is a crossroads of American culture, and one of the fastest-growing areas of the Upper South.

Chapter 4
Wildlife

With so much wooded area throughout the state of Tennessee, it is not uncommon to encounter some kind of wildlife wherever you travel. Wild animals abound, including 66 species of mammals, 200 bird species, 50 types of fish, and over 80 varieties of reptiles.

Rabbits and hares run rampant in the country and the suburbs of Tennessee.

Tennessee is home to over 200 species of birds.

One of the many species of birds found throughout Tennessee.

Over 500 bears can be found inside just the Great Smoky Mountain park alone.

Official Tennessee Animals and Insects

State Bird	Mockingbird
State Wild Animal	Raccoon
State Insects	Firefly and Ladybug
State Butterfly	Zebra Butterfly
State Reptile	Eastern Box Turtle
State Sport Fish	Largemouth Bass
State Commercial Fish	Channel Catfish

Possibly the most popular Smoky Mountain resident, the black bear adult can reach over 400 pounds and can stand over 6 feet tall. Between 500 to 600 bears reside in the Great Smoky Mountain park. Cubs are born during the winter months and mothers venture out of the den with the cubs in March or April. Mother bears are never far from their cubs and are aggressively protective, so visitors should place as much distance as possible between themselves and any cubs they encounter.

The most popular Smoky Mountain resident: the black bear.

The curious white-tailed deer.

Abundant in the state, the white-tailed deer is usually visible in the early-morning hours. Since deer enjoy clearings surrounded by wooded areas, they can be seen easily and regularly.

Deer can commonly be seen n the country and the suburbs of Tennessee

Of the thirty-two snake varieties found in the state, the timber rattlesnake, cottonmouth, water moccasin, and the northern copperhead are the only poisonous ones. One of the most commonly spotted is the gray rat snake, locally known as the "chicken snake."

One of thirty-two snake varieties that can be found throughout the state.

Tennessee Humor

There are 5,000 types of snakes, and 4,998 live in Tennessee.

Watch out for the water moccasin.

This curious snake spies his prey.

The wicked copperhead.

Visitors might also stumble upon a raccoon, opossum, skunk, chipmunk, or a variety of squirrels. The animals are usually harmless when respected and enjoyed from a distance.

Visit with a variety of rodents in the hills of Tennessee.

The official state wild animal: the raccoon.

Chipmunks don't really look much like Alvin!

This little critter will make off with your lunch.

The most common birds seen or heard within the park are the dark-eyed junco, crow, raven, ruffed grouse, and wild turkey. Over 200 species of birds live in Tennessee, about 80 of which remain throughout the winter.

Geese are very common throughout the state.

Adult geese taking their little ones for a morning swim in Percy Priest Lake, Hermitage, Tennessee.

Tennessee Fun Fact

The song of the official state bird, the mockingbird, is, in fact, a medley of the calls of many other birds, each repeated several times. It will imitate other species' songs and calls, squeaky gates, pianos, sirens, barking dogs, etc. Each imitation is repeated two or three times, then another song is started, all in rapid succession. It is common for an individual bird to have as many as twenty-five to thirty songs in its repertory.

Wild turkeys.

The cardinal.

One of many birds that are commonly encountered throughout the state.

The mockingbird.

The American Bald Eagle.

A camouflaged grouse.

The official state commercial fish: the catfish ...

Tennessee Humor

Fried catfish is the other white meat.

Tennessee has plenty of wilderness to enjoy with wildlife as nature intended.

... the other white meat.

Opposum.

71

Beautiful insects abound.

Zebra butterfly.

Chapter 5
Eastern Tennessee

East Tennessee is a region abounding in urban areas, natural beauty, attractions, and athletics. You can traverse the Smoky Mountains or hike a portion of the Appalachian Trail, but if the outdoors are not what you are into, you can cruise into one of the diverse urban areas, including Knoxville, Chattanooga, Bristol, Kingsport, or Johnson City.

Tennessee Fun Fact

Coca-Cola® was first bottled in 1899 at a plant in Chattanooga.

East Tennessee is home to an exceptional list of attractions, including the Chattanooga Choo Choo, the Tennessee Aquarium, Dollywood®, Rock City, Ruby Falls, the Lost Sea, the International Storytelling Center, Ripley's Aquarium, the Knoxville Zoo, Women's Basketball Hall of Fame, the American Museum of Science and Energy, the birthplace of country music, and NASCAR's® home.

Lodging for tourists in the Great Smoky Mountains.

Ski lifts transport tourists in Gatlinburg, Tennessee.

The Great Smoky Mountains ...

While the mountain springs of East Tennessee and the cooler upper elevations of its mountainous areas have long provided a retreat from the region's summertime heat, much of East Tennessee's tourism industry is a result of land conservation movements in the 1920s and 1930s. The Great Smoky Mountains National Park, established in the early 1930s, led to a tourism boom in Blount and Sevier counties, effectively converting the tiny mountain hamlets of Gatlinburg and Pigeon Forge into resort towns.

Gatlinburg, Tennessee ...

One of the most popular locations to visit in Eastern Tennessee is Gatlinburg. It rests on the border of the Great Smoky Mountains National Park along U.S. Highway 441, which connects Gatlinburg to Cherokee, North Carolina, through the national park.

The Bearskin Lodge. Gatlinburg, Tennessee.

Gatlinburg Convention Center. Gatlinburg, Tennessee.

Settled in the early 1800s, Gatlinburg was first named White Oak Flats for the abundant native white oak trees covering the landscape. It is believed a middle-aged widow, Martha Jane Huskey Ogle, was the first official settler there. She traveled to that location with her family to start a new life in what her late-husband described as a "Land of Paradise" in East Tennessee. In 1854, Radford C. Gatlin arrived in White Oak Flats and opened the village's second general store. Controversy soon surrounded him and he was eventually banished from the community. However, the city still bears his name.

The White Oak Flats Cemetery is an old, Smoky Mountain graveyard, established in 1830. It is supposed to have a record of numerous paranormal reports: ghostly lights, apparitions, orbs, and mysterious voices.

White Oak Flat Cemetery.

Ripley's Believe It or Not Museum.

Robert Ripley, founder of Ripley's Believe It or Not (a franchise that deals in bizarre events and items so strange and unusual that people might question the claims), has an extremely strong presence in Gatlinburg. Ripley's Entertainment runs a number of large attractions throughout Gatlinburg, including a state-of-the-art aquarium, motion rides, a haunted house, a museum, mini golf courses, a mirror maze, and even a Guinness museum.

Ripley's Haunted Adventure.

Mysterious Mansion.

"Stumpy" outside of Ripley's Haunted Adventure.

Mysterious Mansion.

Ripley's Aquarium. Gatlinburg, Tennessee.

Gator, Ripley's Aquarium. Gatlinburg, Tennessee.

Jellyfish, Ripley's Aquarium. Gatlinburg, Tennessee.

Seahorse, Ripley's Aquarium. Gatlinburg, Tennessee.

Ripley's Aquarium. Gatlinburg, Tennessee.

Ober Gatlinburg is the only combined ski resort and amusement park in Tennessee. Overlooking Gatlinburg, the resort was established in 1962 and contains a large mall with indoor amusements, a skating rink, snack bars, a full-service lounge, restaurant, and gift and clothing stores. Outside there is an alpine slide, a scenic chairlift to the top of Mount Harrison, and kiddie rides. What was formerly known as the Black Bear Habitat, where visitors could see bears close-up, recently expanded to become the Wildlife Encounter, where, in addition to the bears, there are animals native to the Great Smoky Mountains, such as river otters, opossums, raccoons, turtles, snakes, and flying squirrels. It has eight ski trails and three chair lifts, and is accessible via roads and a gondola from the city strip.

Ober Gatlinburg Ski Resort skylift.

Gatlinburg Fun Fact

The world's largest artificial skiing surface is located at the Ober Gatlinburg Ski Resort. This five-acre artificial ski surface permits skiing in any type of weather.

Animatronic gunslinger. Gatlinburg, Tennessee.

Wonderworks attraction just outside of Gatlinburg in Pigeon Forge, Tennessee.

Animatronic strongman. Gatlinburg, Tennessee.

Dollywood Grist Mill. Pigeon Forge, Tennessee.

Dollywood is a theme park owned by entertainer Dolly Parton and the Herschend Family Entertainment Corporation. It is located in Pigeon Forge, Tennessee.

The park first opened in 1961 as a small tourist attraction by the Robins brothers from Blowing Rock, North Carolina, named "Rebel Railroad," featuring a steam train, general store, blacksmith shop, and saloon. The park was modeled after their first successful theme park "Tweetsie" in Blowing Rock. In 1970, Rebel Railroad was renamed "Goldrush Junction" when it was bought by Art Modell, who also owned the Cleveland Browns football team. In 1976, Jack and Pete Herschend bought Goldrush Junction and renamed it "Goldrush" for the 1976 season. In 1977, they renamed it "Silver Dollar City Tennessee" as a sister park to their original Silver Dollar City in Branson, Missouri.

In 1986, Dolly Parton became a co-owner and the park was renamed "Dollywood." In 2010, Parton said she became involved with the operation because, "I always thought that if I made it big or got successful at what I had started out to do, that I wanted to come back to my part of the country and do something great, something that would bring a lot of jobs into this area."

Dollywood has 3,000 people on its payroll, making it the largest employer in that community.

Tennessee Fun Fact

A common and humorous nickname for Tennessee is "The Dollywood State."

Dollywood coaster. Pigeon Forge, Tennessee ...

In addition to standard amusement park thrill rides, Dollywood features traditional crafts and music of the Smoky Mountains area. Dollywood also owns the adjacent Dollywood's Splash Country and a chain of Dixie Stampede dinner theaters. The park hosts a number of concerts and musical events each year, including appearances by Parton and her family, as well as other national and local musical acts. As of 2010, the park was the biggest "ticketed" tourist attraction in Tennessee each year for more than a decade.

The small city of Oak Ridge holds an important position in the state of Tennessee. Located about twenty-five miles west of Knoxville, Oak Ridge was established in 1942 as a production site for the Manhattan Project: the massive U.S. Government operation that developed the atomic bomb. Scientific development still plays a crucial role in the city's economy and culture in general.

Beginning in October 1942, the United States Army Corps of Engineers began acquiring the Oak Ridge area for the Manhattan Project. Unlike traditional land acquisitions, the Corps' "declaration of

Oak Ridge, Tennessee, power plant.

Tennessee Fun Fact

Oak Ridge, Tennessee, is known as "The Energy Capital Of The World."

Oak Ridge Y12 nuclear facility.

Oak Ridge nuclear reactor.

taking" was much more swift and final. Many residents came home to find eviction notices tacked to their doors. Most were given six weeks to evacuate, although several had as little as two weeks. Some were even forced out before they received compensation.

The location and low population helped keep the town a secret. Although the population of the settlement grew from about 3,000 in 1942 to about 75,000 in 1945, and despite the fact that the K-25 uranium-separating facility by itself covered 44 acres and was the largest building in the world at that time, Oak Ridge was kept an official government secret. It did not appear on maps and wasn't formally named until 1949, only being referred to as the Clinton Engineer Works. All workers wore badges and the town was surrounded by guard towers and a fence with seven gates. Three of the four major facilities created for the wartime bomb production are still standing today.

Ruby Falls is a 145-foot-high underground waterfall located within Lookout Mountain, near Chattanooga, Tennessee. The cave that houses Ruby Falls was formed along with the formation of Lookout Mountain about 200 to 240 million years ago. The eastern Tennessee area was covered with a shallow sea, the sediments of which eventually formed limestone rock. About 200 million years ago, this area was uplifted and subsequent erosion has created the current topography. The limestone in which the cave is formed is still relatively horizontal, just as it was deposited when it was below sea level.

Public tours began in 1930. Electric lights were installed in the cave, making Ruby Falls one of the first commercial caves to be so outfitted and has been designated a National Historic Landmark.

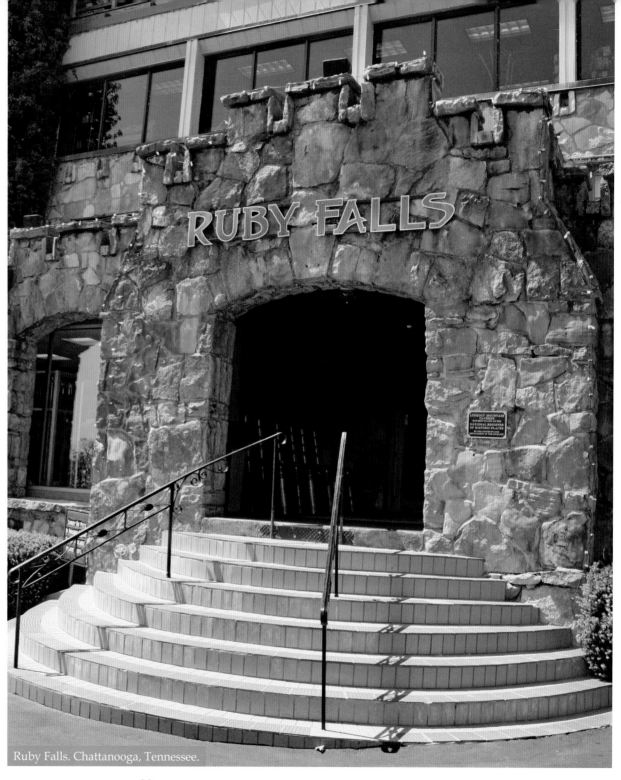

Ruby Falls. Chattanooga, Tennessee.

Ruby Falls. Chattanooga, Tennessee.

Ruby Falls cave system. Chattanooga, Tennessee.

Ruby Falls cave system. Chattanooga, Tennessee.

Ruby Falls cave system. Chattanooga, Tennessee.

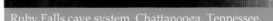

Ruby Falls cave system. Chattanooga, Tennessee.

Ruby Falls Fun Facts

- An all-female American indie rock band called Ruby Falls was active during the 1990s.
- Johnny Cash once recorded "See Ruby Fall," a play on words of Ruby Falls.
- The hard rock band, Mastodon, filmed the performance footage of the music video for their song "Colony of Birchmen" from the album *Blood Mountain* inside Ruby Falls. The waterfall itself can be seen in the background.
- In a television episode titled "The Red Badge of Gayness," in season three of *South Park*, Cartman writes of Kenny's death at "The Battle of Ruby Falls Funland."

Rock City is a roadside attraction near Chattanooga, Tennessee, on Lookout Mountain located near Ruby Falls. Although, technically, this is an attraction in the state of Georgia, most Tennessee residents and travelers consider it a Tennessee attraction. It is well-known for the many barn advertisements throughout the Southeast and Midwest United States that have the slogan "See Rock City" painted on barn roofs and sides. In total, over 900 barn roofs in 19 states were painted by Clark Byers for Rock City.

The publicity and lore claim that it is possible to see seven states from Lover's Leap, a point in Rock City, but this has not been proven scientifically. By the time the American Civil War reached the slopes of Lookout Mountain, more and more people had discovered what was already, at that time, being called the Rock City. During the Battle of Lookout Mountain, both a Union and a Confederate claimed that seven states could be seen from the summit of the mountain.

Rock City was opened as a public attraction in 1932.

Lover's Leap at Rock City.

See seven states at once at Lover's Leap, Rock City.

Rock City Fun Facts

- The Rock City vista is the site of the climax of Neil Gaiman's 2001 novel *American Gods*.
- The main characters in Cormac McCarthy's novel *The Road*, while traveling in a post-apocalyptic world in an unnamed U.S. state, pass a barn advertising "See Rock City."
- Bela Fleck's album Drive contains an original banjo instrumental entitled "See Rock City."

A close-up shot of the waterfall at Lover's Leap at Rock City.

Bluff View Art District. Chattanooga, Tennessee.

Bluff View Art District, dedicated to the visual, horticultural, and culinary arts, is a historic neighborhood in Chattanooga filled with restaurants, a coffee house, art gallery, historic bed and breakfast, and plenty of gardens, plazas, and courtyards to relax in. This is Chattanooga's first art district and stretches over 1.5 city blocks, set high atop stone cliffs that plunge into the river below. From this bluff-top location, visitors can get a great view of the Tennessee River, downtown Chattanooga, and the Walnut Street Bridge.

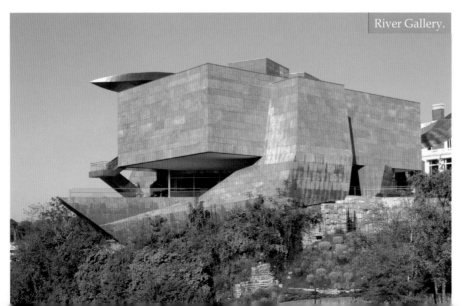
River Gallery.

Outdoor sculptures ...

94

The River Gallery features nationally recognized artists and is frequented by working artists who hold classes and demonstrations for the public weekly. Master gardeners tend to the Bluff View Art District's landscaping features, including the award-winning River Gallery Sculpture Garden, duly noted by the Smithsonian in its Archive of American Gardens.

Terminal Station in Chattanooga, Tennessee, is a former railroad station, once owned and operated by the Southern Railway. The station was opened in 1909 and was the latest and largest station in Chattanooga's history. The Beaux-Arts-style station, designed by Donn Barber, was one of the grandest buildings in Chattanooga, featuring an arched main entrance that claims to be the largest unsupported brick arch in the world. The building also has an eighty-two-foot-high ceiling dome with a skylight in the center section.

Terminal Station, Chattanooga, Tennessee…

Terminal Station, Chattanooga, Tennessee.

The world-famous Chattanooga Choo-Choo!

The 1941 Glenn Miller song "Chattanooga Choo Choo" told the story of a train trip from Pennsylvania Station, in New York City, through Baltimore, North and South Carolina, and terminating at Track 29 in Terminal Station.

As the railroad industry declined in the 1950s and 1960s, passenger traffic dwindled and the last passenger train, *The Birmingham Special*, left Terminal Station in 1970. In 1972, local businessmen bought the building, renamed it the Chattanooga Choo-Choo, after the song, and began rehabilitating the building. Today, the twenty-four-acre complex is a convention center, hotel, and resort with restaurants and shops.

Actual Tennessee Law

No Christian parent may require their children to pick up trash from the highway on Easter day.

Welcome to Chattanooga, Tennessee.

Industry in Chattanooga.

Incline Railway.

The Lookout Mountain Incline Railway is an inclined plane railway located along the side of Lookout Mountain in Chattanooga. Passengers are transported from St. Elmo's Station, at the base, to Point Park, at the mountain summit, which overlooks the city and the Tennessee River. The railway is approximately one mile in length and has a maximum grade of 72.7%. It is billed as the world's steepest passenger railway.

The Incline Railway opened on November 16, 1895, and was the second of two inclines constructed on Lookout Mountain; the first was the Chattanooga and Lookout Mountain Railway, which operated from 1886 to 1898. The railway is now operated by the Chattanooga Area Regional Transportation Authority, the area's public transit agency.

Founded in 1786, Knoxville is the third-largest city in the state of Tennessee, behind Memphis and Nashville, and is the county seat of Knox County. It is the largest city in East Tennessee and the second-largest city (behind Pittsburgh) in the Appalachia region.

Of Tennessee's four major cities, Knoxville is second oldest to Nashville, which was founded seven years earlier. After Tennessee's admission into the Union in 1796, Knoxville was the state's first capital. In 1819, the capital was moved to Murfreesboro, prior to Nashville receiving the designation. The city was named in honor of the first Secretary of War, Henry Knox.

Knoxville is the home of the University of Tennessee's flagship campus. The university's sports teams, called the "Volunteers" or "Vols," are extremely popular in the surrounding area. In recognition of this popularity, the telephone area code for Knox County and eight adjacent counties is 865 (VOL).

Knoxville, Tennessee.

Knoxville Fun Fact

Knoxville was once known as the "Underwear Capital of the World." In the 1930s, no fewer than twenty textile and clothing mills operated in Knoxville, and the industry was the city's largest employer.

Knoxville skyline.

Knoxville, Tennessee, Sunsphere from the 1982 World's Fair.

Knoxville, Tennessee.

White's Fort.

White's Fort, also known as James White's Fort, was an eighteenth-century settlement that became Knoxville, Tennessee. The settlement of White's Fort began in 1786 by James White, a militia officer during the American Revolutionary War. The fort itself began when James White built a cabin near what is now the corner of State Street and Clinch Avenue. This cabin soon became the center of a cluster of fortified log structures known as White's Fort.

The Blount Mansion, located in downtown Knoxville, was the home of the only territorial governor of the Southwest Territory, William Blount (1749–1800). Blount, also a signer of the United States Constitution and a U.S. Senator from Tennessee, lived on the property with his family and ten African Americans. Along with Blount's residence, the mansion served

Bleak House.

Blount Mansion.

as the de facto capitol of the Southwest Territory, and in 1796, much of the Tennessee Constitution was drafted at the mansion. Tennessee state historian John Trotwood Moore once called Blount Mansion "the most important historical spot in Tennessee."

The house is a wood-frame home sheathed in wood siding, built with materials brought from North Carolina in an era when most homes in Tennessee were log cabins. The two-story central portion of the home is the oldest section. The one-story east wing is believed to have been constructed next; archaeologists suspect the east wing was originally an outbuilding, which was then moved and attached to the main house, and there is some evidence the east wing was originally the servants' quarters. The one-story west wing was the final section to be constructed, perhaps as late as 1820. Blount's office, from which he governed and conducted his business affairs, was built along with the house and is a one-story, free-standing building with a modest front porch.

Bleak House is an antebellum Classical Revival style house in Knoxville. The house was first occupied by Robert Houston Armstrong and his wife, Louisa Franklin. It was built for the couple as a wedding gift by the bride's father, Major L.D. Franklin. Robert Armstrong's father, Drury Armstrong, gave them the land. The Armstrongs named the house after Charles Dickens' *Bleak House* novel of the same name. The bricks in the house were molded on-site using slave labor.

The home was used by Confederate Generals James Longstreet and Lafayette McLaws as their headquarters during the 1863 Battle of Knoxville. Three Confederate sharpshooters who were stationed in the house's tower were killed by Union cannonballs. Two of the cannonballs are still embedded in the walls, and Civil War-era sketches of the slain soldiers are displayed on the walls of the tower.

The home now belongs to local Chapter 89 of the United Daughters of the Confederacy and is commonly called Confederate Memorial Hall.

With all of this, and more, eastern Tennessee offers a little something for everyone.

Bleak House.

"It is well that war is so terrible, else we should grow too fond of it."
— General Robert E. Lee

The Civil War has always been one of my favorite time periods in history. It enthralls me while, at the same time, it confuses and frustrates me. So, it should be of no surprise that I find battle sites in Tennessee some of the most interesting places to visit.

Tennessee was host to some of the most brutal and bloody battles of the Civil War. Tennessee sided with the South in the sectional controversy preceding the American Civil War but tried to avoid secession, giving its electoral vote to the Constitutional Union Party in the crucial election of 1880. When hostilities broke out between the North and the South the following year, though, Tennessee went into the Confederacy.

More Civil War battles were fought in Tennessee than in any other state except Virginia. The state was a principal battleground in the War Between the States. Major battles were fought at Fort Donelson, Shiloh, Murfreesboro, Chattanooga, Franklin, and Nashville, making Tennessee a great tourist location for historians and Civil War buffs from around the globe.

Civil War re-enactments are abundant in Tennessee.

A Confederate soldier watches over the battlefield.

Confederate camp.

The Battle of Franklin, one of the bloodiest battles of the war, took place just a short distance from Nashville and attracts thousands of tourists per year to the location and the two plantation houses, which sit on each end of the battlefield — the Carter House and the Carnton Mansion.

The small town of Franklin had been a Union military post since the fall of Nashville in early 1862. Late in the summer of 1864, Confederate President Jefferson Davis placed General John Bell Hood in charge of the Army of Tennessee. Hood immediately began to formulate a plan to drive the Union army away from Atlanta and Robert E. Lee's forces.

Under Hood's command, the Army of Tennessee moved north through Georgia, Alabama, and then into Columbia, Tennessee, flanking the Union forces. They forced the Yankees, under the command of General Schofield, to flee. Schofield desperately needed to join the ranks with General Thomas at Nashville, but to do this he had to get past Hood.

Somehow, under the cover of night, Schofield was able to slip past Hood and move further north into Franklin, Tennessee. As the Yankees arrived in Franklin, General Cox commandeered the Carter House as a command post.

Author Jim O'Rear in Confederate garb for the movie *Shudder*.

Abe Lincoln prepares an address.

Confederate camp.

The land around the Carter house became a human slaughtering pen. It was such a bad situation that the Battle of Franklin has been called "the bloodiest hours of the American Civil War" and is referred to as "The Gettysburg of the West." It was one of the few night battles in the War Between the States and, also, one of the smallest battlefields (only two miles long and one and a half miles wide).

War cemetery.

When Hood found out that he had been outmaneuvered, he marched his men in pursuit of the Federal troops. Hood was determined to destroy the Union army before it reached Nashville. The Army of Tennessee knew the assault on the town of Franklin would be suicidal, but they bravely advanced toward town and the Carter House with their heads held high.

In the late afternoon of November 30, 1864, Hood's men charged the Federal troops. The fighting was brutal and fiendishly savage, with men bayoneted and clubbed to death in the Carter yard. Soldiers were clawing, punching, stabbing, and choking each other to death. The smoke from the cannons and guns was so thick that they couldn't tell friend from foe.

A lonely monument to a lost Civil War soldier.

Tennessee Civil War Fun Fact

The only monument in the United States honoring BOTH the Union and Confederate armies is located in Greenville, Tennessee, at the Green County Courthouse.

One of many Civil War monuments scattered throughout the battlefields of Tennessee

As previously mentioned, the other structure that stands on the small battlefield, the Carnton Mansion, has been called the "most haunted building in Tennessee" and is now the final resting-place of over 1,480 soldiers. As battle erupted around the Carnton Mansion, more than 200 injured soldiers were brought inside, where the owners tried to do anything that they could to help them. Doctors operated in the parlor and the dead were carried out and stacked on the back porch until there was no more room. The floors of the mansion are still stained with the blood of the dying soldiers.

The Carnton Mansion. Franklin, Tennessee ...

The Carnton Mansion. Franklin, Tennessee.

To
The memory of
JAMES T. SMITH,

A Union monument stands on a hill overlooking Chattanooga, Tennessee.

Tennessee Civil War Fun Fact

Tennessee was the last state to secede from the Union during the Civil War and the first state to be readmitted after the war.

The sheer amount of history contained in the three-mile stretch of land that encompassed the Battle of Franklin makes this location a must see while traveling in Tennessee.

Another noteworthy stop for Civil War buffs is the Chickamauga battlefield. The year of 1863 was a triumphant one for the Union army. Led to many victories by General Ulysses S. Grant, the Union forces were cocky and confident. They had no doubt that they could achieve another great victory in Chattanooga, Tennessee.

Located above the bend of the Tennessee River in the southeastern corner of the state, Chattanooga was the junction point of two important railroad lines. Many considered it to be the "gateway to the Confederacy." If the Union could capture this region then they could move south into Georgia and divide the Confederacy.

Union General Rosecrans commanded the attack, executing a series of flanking maneuvers that pushed the Confederate commander Bragg back more than eighty miles. Unfortunately for Rosecrans, Rebel reinforcements, under the command of General Longstreet, arrived by train and lured the Union army away from Chattanooga to Chickamauga Creek. Bragg and Longstreet battered the Union forces relentlessly until

Chickamauga Battlefield ...

Rosecrans made a fatal error. Rosecrans accidentally ordered his men to close a gap in the Union line that did not exist. In doing this, he actually created a hole that Longstreet charged through, devastating the Yankee troops.

The Battle of Chickamauga was brutal, lasting two days and claiming more than 35,000 lives. The Confederates won the day, but it would turn out to be one of the last major Rebel victories of the war.

Chickamauga also has a lot of ghost stories associated with it, but that's a completely different book.

After the September 1862 battle of Chickamauga, Confederate troops occupied Lookout Mountain. By securing Lookout Mountain, Missionary Ridge, and the valley between, the Confederates held the Federals in Chattanooga.

Robert Cravens, a leading industrialist in Chattanooga, had purchased a thousand acres of land on the side of Lookout Mountain, where he maintained an orchard and built several cabins as a summer retreat for his family. Confederate forces built defenses that passed through Cravens's land, making the house a target for the Federal artillery on Moccasin Bend. Although the house was struck six times, the family remained until mid-November.

On November 24, 1863, General Joseph Hooker and his Union troops attacked Lookout Mountain, which became known as "The Battle Above the Clouds." The Confederates made stubborn resistance at the house but retreated by mid-afternoon. Once in the possession of the Union troops, Cravens's house became the headquarters for General W. C. Whitaker's command.

The beautiful Cravens House. Chattanooga, Tennessee.

The Cravens House. Chattanooga, Tennessee.

The Cravens House. Chattanooga, Tennessee ...

Civil War cemetery.

Although the house sustained little damage during the battle, Union soldiers destroyed the house afterwards during a drunken brawl. Only the base of the home and a nearby outbuilding remained. The Cravens returned to rebuild and live in it after the war.

Of course, volumes could be filled on the historic Civil War locations throughout Tennessee and their significance in history, but this is a travel book, after all. There are many more fantastic locations similar to these, so I hope that this sample has whet your appetite.

Civil War fort.

Industry 1800s style.

Typical living conditions for Tennesseans during the Civil War.

Living conditions were not the greatest during the Civil War.

Slave cabin.

Chapter 7
Western Tennessee

"I'll stay in Memphis."
– Elvis Presley

West Tennessee offers a variety of historic locations and sites to experience. The whole feeling, atmosphere, and look of west Tennessee is very different than anywhere else in the state. That side of Tennessee emits a totally unique vibe. Although there is plenty to see and experience in the western part of the state, my primary focus in this book will be the Memphis area, mainly due to the number of historic events and residents in that area and the cultural significance it lends to the state as a whole.

Memphis had a population of 646,889 at the 2010 census, making it the biggest city in the state of Tennessee, the third largest in the Southeastern United States, and the twentieth largest in the United States. This also makes Memphis the second largest metropolitan area in Tennessee, surpassed only by metropolitan Nashville, which has overtaken Memphis in recent years. Memphis is the youngest of Tennessee's major cities.

Because it occupies a substantial bluff rising from the Mississippi River, the site of Memphis was a natural location for settlement. The area was first settled by the Mississippian culture and then by the Chickasaw Indian tribe. For 10,000 years they occupied the bluffs along the river.

Downtown Memphis, Tennessee.

A typical high-rise found just outside of Memphis, Tennessee.

Memphis was founded in 1819 by John Overton, James Winchester, and Andrew Jackson. The city was named after the ancient capital of Egypt on the Nile River. Memphis developed as a transportation center in the nineteenth century because of its flood-free location, high above the Mississippi River. As the cotton economy of the antebellum South depended on the forced labor of large numbers of African American slaves, Memphis became a major slave market. In 1857, the Memphis and Charleston Railroad was completed, the only east-west railroad across the southern states prior to the Civil War.

In the 1870s, a series of yellow fever epidemics devastated Memphis. The worst outbreak, in 1878, reduced the population by nearly 75% as many people died or fled the city permanently. Property tax revenues collapsed and the city could not make payments on its municipal debts. As a result, Memphis temporarily lost its city charter and was a taxing district from 1878-1893. The city was rechartered in 1893.

Apartment living in downtown Memphis, Tennessee.

As evident in this establishment's sign, civil rights still remain an issue in Memphis, Tennessee.

Actual Tennessee Law

In Memphis, it is illegal for frogs to croak after 11 p.m.

Fancy hotels like this one stand in stark contrast to some of the sub-standard living conditions found in the Memphis area.

Part of the nightlife in west Tennessee.

Establishments overgrown with trees, weeds, and kudzoo are common in west Tennessee.

Graceland, home of The King. Memphis, Tennessee ...

Entry gates to Graceland.

The walls outside Graceland are covered with notes from fans.

Memphis grew into the world's largest spot cotton market and the world's largest hardwood lumber market. Into the 1950s, it was the world's largest mule market.

Of course, one of Memphis' most famous and influential residents was "The King of Rock and Roll," Elvis Presley, who established his home, known as Graceland, in the city.

Graceland is a large, white-columned mansion and 13.8-acre estate that was home to Elvis Presley, in Memphis. It is located about nine miles from downtown and less than four miles north of the Mississippi border. It was opened to the public on June 7, 1982. Graceland has become one of the most-visited private homes in America with over 600,000 visitors a year, behind the White House and Biltmore Estate (900,000 visitors per year).

Elvis Presley died at the estate on August 16, 1977. Presley, his parents Gladys and Vernon Presley, and his grandmother are buried there, in what is called the Meditation Garden.

The mansion is constructed of tan limestone and consists of twenty-three rooms, including eight bedrooms and bathrooms. The entrance way contains four Temple of the Winds columns and two large lions perched on both sides of the portico.

Inside Graceland ....

Elvis' grave.

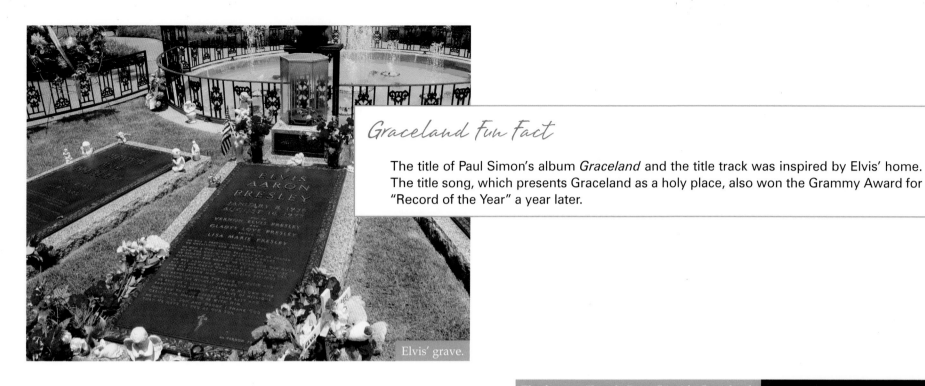

Elvis' grave.

Graceland Fun Fact

The title of Paul Simon's album *Graceland* and the title track was inspired by Elvis' home. The title song, which presents Graceland as a holy place, also won the Grammy Award for "Record of the Year" a year later.

After purchasing the property, Presley carried out extensive modifications to suit his needs and tastes, including: a fieldstone wall surrounding the grounds, a wrought-iron music-themed gate, a swimming pool, a racquetball court, and the famous "Jungle Room," which features an indoor waterfall, among other modifications. In February and October 1976, the Jungle Room was converted into a recording studio, where Presley recorded the bulk of his final two albums, "From Elvis Presley Boulevard, Memphis, Tennessee" and "Moody Blue."

The famous "Jungle Room" inside Graceland.

Elvis' billiard room ....

Elvis' television room.

In 1890, the Grand Opera House was built on the corner of Main and Beale Street. The Grand was billed as the classiest theater outside of New York City. Vaudeville was the main source of entertainment at the time. The Grand became part of the Orpheum Vaudeville circuit in 1907 and was renamed the Orpheum Theater.

The Orpheum is one of Memphis' most incredible success stories—a theater able to overcome a variety of hardships that ranged from several bankruptcies, a devastating fire, the decay of downtown Memphis, and the threat of demolition for the construction of an office complex. Vaudeville at the Orpheum was successful for almost twenty years, but, in 1923, a fire broke out during a show that featured a striptease artist named Blossom Seeley and burned the structure to the ground.

In 1928, a new Orpheum was built upon the same site for 1.6 million dollars. It was twice as large as the original. This new brick building houses a five-floor theater with over 2,500 seats and features a high ceiling supporting 2,000-pound chandeliers, ornamental plaster work, gold leafing, lavish tasseled brocade draperies, and a large Wurlitzer pipe organ. Nicknamed the "South's Finest Theater," the Orpheum is one of the few remaining movie palaces of the 1920s. It is also said to be haunted by seven ghosts.

The Orpheum. Memphis, Tennessee.

The Orpheum in Memphis announces its Broadway season.

Actual Tennessee Law

Panhandlers must first obtain a $10 permit before begging on the streets of downtown Memphis.

The King's Heartbreak Hotel left many heartbroken when it closed down.

Beale Street is a street in Downtown Memphis that runs from the Mississippi River to East Street, a distance of approximately 1.8 miles. Beale Street was created in 1841 by entrepreneur and developer Robertson Topp, who named it for a forgotten military hero. Its western end primarily housed shops of trade merchants, who traded goods with ships along the Mississippi River, while the eastern part developed as an affluent suburb. In the 1860s, many black traveling musicians began performing on Beale. It became a recreational and cultural center, where blues musicians could gather, and earned the nickname "The Birthplace of the Blues."

Get your beer on Beale Street.

Beale Street. Memphis, Tennessee...

On December 15, 1977, Beale Street was officially declared the "Home of the Blues" by an act of Congress. Despite this national recognition of its historic significance, Beale was a virtual ghost town after a disastrous urban renewal program with every building, except Schwabs, boarded up. It was not until the 1980s that Beale Street was redeveloped by Elkington & Keltnerr, which led to an economic revitalization with new clubs and attractions opening.

Beale Street. Memphis, Tennessee.

World-famous Sun Studio. Memphis, Tennessee.

140

Tennessee Humor

Tea is appropriate for all meals and you start drinking it when you are two years of age.

Sun Studio is a recording studio opened by rock pioneer Sam Phillips in Memphis on January 3, 1950. It was originally called Memphis Recording Service, sharing the same building with the Sun Records label business. Reputedly, the first rock-and-roll single, Jackie Brenston and his Delta Cats' "Rocket 88" was recorded there in 1951 with song composer Ike Turner on keyboards, leading the studio to claim status as "The Birthplace of Rock-and-Roll."

Blues and R&B artists like Howlin' Wolf, Junior Parker, Little Milton, B.B. King, James Cotton, Rufus Thomas, and Rosco Gordon recorded there in the early 1950s. Rock-and-roll, country music, and rockabilly artists, including Johnny Cash, Elvis Presley, Carl Perkins, Roy Orbison, Charlie Feathers, Ray Harris, Warren Smith, Charlie Rich, and Jerry Lee Lewis, recorded there throughout the mid to late 1950s until the studio outgrew its Union Avenue location.

Inside Sun Studio ...

The Memphis Pyramid.

One of the most unique structures in Tennessee is The Pyramid Arena, a 20,142-seat arena located in downtown Memphis at the banks of the Mississippi River. The facility was built in 1991. It is 321 feet tall (about 32 stories) and has base sides of 591 feet. It is the sixth largest pyramid in the world behind the Great Pyramid of Giza, Khafre's Pyramid, Luxor Hotel, the Red Pyramid, and the Bent Pyramid. It is also slightly (about sixteen feet) taller than the Statue of Liberty. A statue of Ramesses the Great stands in front of the pyramid.

It was the home court for the University of Memphis men's basketball program and, later, for the National Basketball Association's Memphis Grizzlies. However, both teams left The Pyramid in November 2004 to move into the newly built FedEx Forum.

Filmmaker Craig Brewer used the building as a sound stage for his film *Black Snake Moan* in late 2005.

Bob Seger and The Silver Bullet Band performed, what is reputed to be, the last concert ever in the Pyramid on February 3, 2007.

When the FedEx Forum overtook the Pyramid as the city's primary indoor sports arena, the Pyramid did not have any long-term tenants. In 2005, a committee studied possible uses of the arena and considered uses such as converting the arena into a casino, an aquarium, a shopping center, or an indoor theme park. In November 2006, Congressman-Elect Steve Cohen suggested that he would attempt to open a "Mid-American branch" of the Smithsonian Institution in the building. However, none of these plans were ever realized.

After five years of negotiating, Bass Pro and the City of Memphis signed an agreement for a fifty-five-year lease which would create a Bass Pro Shop store, additional retail stores, restaurants, offices, and a river museum. In addition, the redevelopment plans included revitalizing the Pinch District, which is the neighborhood around the Pyramid. The city would invest thirty million dollars to help with the seismic retrofitting of the structure, which would be funded by future sales tax revenue in the surrounding area. Bass Pro was to begin renovations and construction in October 2011 for an opening in August 2013.

FedEx Forum. Memphis, Tennessee.

Sporting area on the edge of town that helps make up the Memphis skyline.

The National Civil Rights Museum in Memphis is a privately owned complex of museums and historic buildings built around the former Lorraine Motel, where Martin Luther King, Jr. was assassinated on April 4, 1968.

Major components of the complex on the 4.14 acres include a museum which traces the history of the Civil Rights Movement from the 1600s to the present, the Lorraine Motel, as well as the Young and Morrow Building (up a small hill across the street from the motel), which was the site where James Earl Ray initially confessed (and later recanted) to shooting King from a second-story bathroom window, as well as the Canipe's Amusement Store where the alleged murder weapon with Ray's fingerprints was found. Included on the grounds is the brushy lot that stood between the rooming house and the motel. It is on this lot where an alternate theory states that the fatal shot came from a different weapon at ground level. This conspiracy theory involves Loyd Jowers, who operated Jim's Grill, which opened onto the lot.

Actual Tennessee Law

In Dyersburg, located in west Tennessee, it is illegal for a woman to call a man for a date.

The Lorraine Motel. Memphis, Tennessee.

The Lorraine Motel, where Martin Luther King Jr. was assassinated.

The first hotel on the site was the sixteen-room Windsor Hotel, built on the northern side of the complex around 1925, which was renamed the Marquette Hotel. Walter Bailey purchased it in 1945 and renamed it for his wife, Loree, and the song "Sweet Lorraine." During segregation it was an upscale accommodation that catered to a black clientele. He added a second floor and then drive-up access for more rooms on the south side of the complex, changing the name from Lorraine Hotel to Lorraine Motel. Its guests included musicians, such as Ray Charles, Lionel Hampton, Aretha Franklin, Ethel Waters, Otis Redding, and Wilson Pickett.

Following the assassination of Martin Luther King, Jr., Bailey left Room 306, outside of which King was assassinated, and the adjoining room 307 unoccupied as a memorial to King. Bailey's wife, Loree, who suffered a stroke hours after the assassination, died five days later.

The Lorraine Motel had not only guests, but residents as well. The last resident of the motel, Jacqueline Smith, had resided there since 1973 as part of her work for the motel as a housekeeper. When faced with eviction for the museum project, Smith barricaded herself in her room and had to be forcibly evicted.

The Lorraine closed as a motel on March 2, 1988, when sheriff's deputies evicted Smith, in preparation for an $8.8 million overhaul. Smith stated that the Lorraine "should be put to better uses, such as housing, job training, free college, clinic, or other services for the poor... The area surrounding the Lorraine should be rejuvenated and made decent and kept affordable, not gentrified with expensive condominiums that price the people out of their community." She has also stated that

Dr. King would not have wanted $9 million spent on a building for him, and would not have wanted Lorraine Motel residents to be evicted.

Apparently, this entire incident really angered Smith as she has maintained an irate vigil across the street from the Lorraine Motel for up to twenty-one hours per day ever since her eviction, regardless of weather.

The museum was dedicated on July 4, 1991, and officially opened to the public on September 28, 1991.

In 1999, the Foundation acquired the Young and Morrow Building and its associated vacant lot on the hill. A tunnel was built under the lot connecting it to the motel. The Foundation became the custodian of the police and evidence files associated with the assassination, including the rifle and fatal bullet which are on display in a 12,800-square-foot exhibit in the building, which opened September 28, 2002.

The largest earthquake in American history, the New Madrid Earthquake, occurred in the winter of 1811-12 in west Tennessee. Reelfoot Lake and Lake Counties were created during this earthquake. Reelfoot Lake is a shallow body of water, much of it being more of a swamp, with bayou-like ditches. Several eyewitnesses reported that the Mississippi River flowed backward for ten to twenty-four hours to fill the lake, but it is most likely that waves from the quake caused the river to appear to flow upstream.

In the early twentieth century, the Reelfoot area was marked by widespread lawlessness and "Night Riding," which resulted in the deployment of the state militia by governor of Tennessee Malcolm R. Patterson. The troubles began when a group of landowners purchased almost the entire

Jacqueline Smith would not allow us to take her picture, but this is where she stages her on-going protest.

Tennessee Humor

You know you're from Tennessee when you find 100 degrees Fahrenheit "a little warm."

The balcony where Martin Luther King, Jr. was assassinated. Memphis, Tennessee.

Reelfoot Lake.

Elvis Presley statue near Beale Street.

Reelfoot Lake Fun Fact

Reelfoot Lake was the location for three memorable Hollywood movie productions: *Raintree County*, the 1957 drama about the American Civil War, starring Elizabeth Taylor, Montgomery Clift, Eva Marie Saint, and Lee Marvin; the 1967 Oscar-winner, *In the Heat of the Night*, starring Sidney Poitier and Best Actor Rod Steiger; and *U.S. Marshals*, the 1998 action thriller, starring Tommy Lee Jones and Wesley Snipes.

shoreline of the lake. They formed the West Tennessee Land Company to enforce what they saw to be their legal rights, including the ownership of the lake itself, and, most importantly, its fishing rights. Most of the Night Riders were from families that had derived much of their living from fishing the lake for generations, joined by their friends and supporters. Two attorneys engaged by the West Tennessee Land Company to enforce its claims were seized by the Night Riders. A contemporary front-page account in the Nashville Banner tells that one lawyer was murdered by being hanged and then shot, while the other escaped by swimming across the lake in the dark while being shot

at by Night Riders. This violence, in 1908, caused the governor to call out the militia to restore order. The murderers were caught, tried, and punished, but the lake was soon declared to be part of the public domain, which guaranteed the right of the public to use it regardless of who owned the land adjacent to it. A system of parks, wildlife refuges, recreation areas, and public boat ramps were eventually developed through federal-state cooperation.

Anyone wanting to experience a wide mixture of culture and lifestyles will be extremely happy after spending just a couple of days in western Tennessee.

"A religion without the element of mystery would not be a religion at all."

— Edwin Lewis

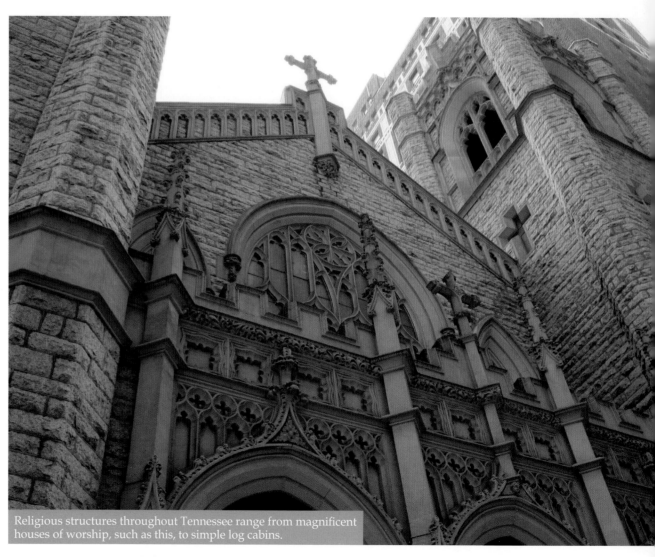

Since its founding as a state in the late eighteenth century until the present, Tennessee has played an active role in American religious history. As part of the western frontier, the state featured prominently in the religious awakenings of the early nineteenth century. Revivals and camp meetings brought evangelical Protestantism to the Tennessee frontier. Other religious groups and denominations existed in Tennessee, such as Quakers, Mormons, and Calvinists, but by the end of the nineteenth century, the Presbyterians, Cumberland Presbyterians, Methodists, and Baptists dominated. During the first part of the twentieth century, Nashville became a central location for religious publishing. As a centerpiece of the southern Bible Belt, Tennessee remains a hotbed of religious activity, publishing, and change.

"Bible Belt" is an informal term for an area of the United States in which socially conservative evangelical Protantism is a significant part of the culture and Christian church attendance across the denominations is generally higher than the nation's average.

The Bible Belt consists of much of the Southern United States extending west into Texas and Oklahoma. During the colonial period (1607–1776), the South was

Religious structures throughout Tennessee range from magnificent houses of worship, such as this, to simple log cabins.

Historic house of worship overlooking South Pittsburg, Tennessee.

a stronghold of the Anglican church. Its transition to a stronghold of non-Anglican Protestantism occurred gradually over the next century as a series of religious revival movements, many associated with the Baptist denomination, gained great popularity in the region.

Nashville, Tennessee, sometimes referred to as The Protestant Vatican, has over 700 churches, several seminaries, and a number of Christian schools, colleges, and universities, including Belmont University, Trevecca Nazarene University, Lipscomb University, Free Will Baptist Bible College, and American Baptist College. Nashville is the seat of the National Baptist Convention, USA; the National Association of Free Will Baptists; the Gideons International; the Gospel

Beautiful Mt. Olivett Cemetery in Nashville, Tennessee.

Tennessee Fun Fact

Religion in Tennessee: 82% Christian (64% Protestant, 6% Catholic, 12% Other), 9% No Religion, 3% Other Religions.

Churches are common found nestled in the middle of busy downtown districts in Tennessee

Music Association; and Thomas Nelson, the world's largest producer of Bibles. It is also the headquarters for the publishing arms of both the Southern Baptist Convention (LifeWay Christian Resources) and the United Methodist Church (United Methodist Publishing House), as well as a number of Christian record companies, such as EMI Christian Music Group, Provident Label Group, and Word Records.

You can get your pets blessed!

Faith is strong in Tennessee. Even when their home was destroyed, this family still held on to their beliefs.

I find it interesting that the lives of many Southerners, especially in Tennessee, are guided by their religion. It is one of the only locations that I have personally witnessed prayer in public school, blowing away the practice of the separation of church and state law. I also find it interesting that residents holding such strong religious convictions would primarily gravitate toward the Baptist religion, in Tennessee. *Why?* you ask. Because of all the religions established in the United States, the Baptist religion is the most varied and most fractured in their beliefs. I would expect people of strong religious convictions to be drawn to more structured religions, such as Catholicism.

Jesus *and* Santa?

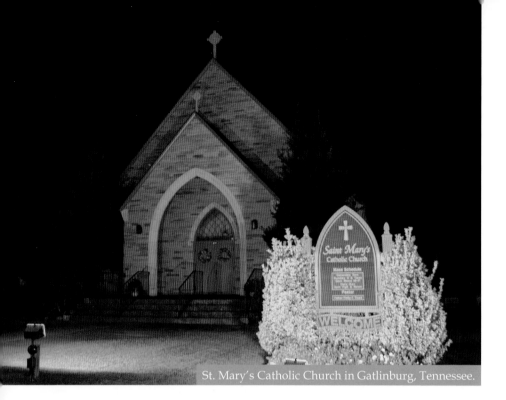

St. Mary's Catholic Church in Gatlinburg, Tennessee.

I don't want this to become a book about religion, but since this book is meant to give the reader the flavor of Tennessee, I'd like to take a moment to discuss the primary religion in the area to provide a better understanding of the people who live there.

Baptists are individuals who belong to Christian denominations and churches that subscribe to a doctrine that baptism should be performed only for professing believers (believer's baptism, as opposed to infant baptism), and that it must be done by immersion (as opposed to affusion or sprinkling). Other tenets of Baptist churches

Statue of Joseph.

Marble mausoleum in east Tennessee.

include soul competency (liberty), salvation through faith alone, scripture alone as the rule of faith and practice, and the autonomy of the local congregation. Baptists recognize two ministerial offices, pastors and deacons. Baptist churches are widely considered to be Protestant churches, though some Baptists disavow this identity.

Diverse from their beginning, those identifying as Baptists today differ widely from one another in what they believe, how they worship, their attitudes toward other Christians, and their understanding of what is important in Christian discipleship.

Historians trace the earliest Baptist church back to 1609 in Amsterdam, with English Separatist John Smyth as its pastor. In accordance with his reading of the New Testament, he rejected baptism of infants and instituted baptism only of believing adults.

In 1638, Roger Williams established the first Baptist congregation in the North American colonies. In the mid-eighteenth century, the First Great Awakening increased Baptist growth in both New England and the South. The Second Great Awakening in the South, in the early nineteenth century, increased church membership, as did the preachers' lessening of support for abolition and manumission of slavery, which had been part of the eighteenth-century teachings. Baptists became the largest Christian community in many southern states, including the black population.

In 1845, the Baptist congregations in the United States split over three main issues: slavery, missions, and doctrinal integrity. The northern congregations were opposed to members in the southern congregations owning slaves and tried to prevent slaveholders from being missionaries. However, not appointing a proportionate number of missionaries to the southern

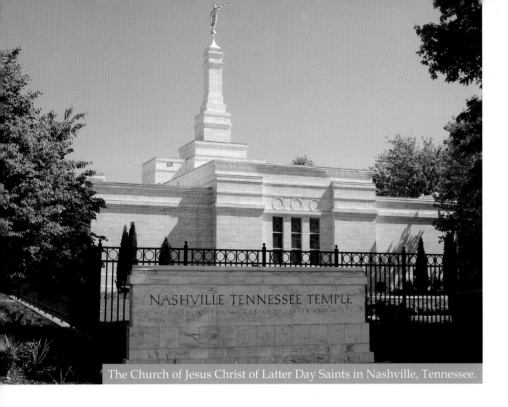

The Church of Jesus Christ of Latter Day Saints in Nashville, Tennessee.

region of the U.S. sparked animosity from the southern churches. The southern congregations were also concerned over perceived liberalism in the north, accusing some missionaries of denying virgin birth and divinity of Jesus. The split created the Southern Baptist Convention, while the northern congregations, then known as Northern Baptists, formed their own umbrella organization, now called the American Baptist Churches of the USA.

After the American Civil War, another split occurred: Most black Baptists in the South separated from white churches and set up their own congregations. In the late 1860s, they rapidly set up several separate state conventions. In 1895, their three national conventions merged into the National Baptist Convention. With eight million members, it is the largest African American religious organization and is second in size to the Southern Baptist Convention, both operating out of the Nashville area.

Tennesseans hold strong religious convictions and those convictions show in every area of their lifestyle.

Some churches prefer to set up shop and worship in shopping strips through Tennessee.

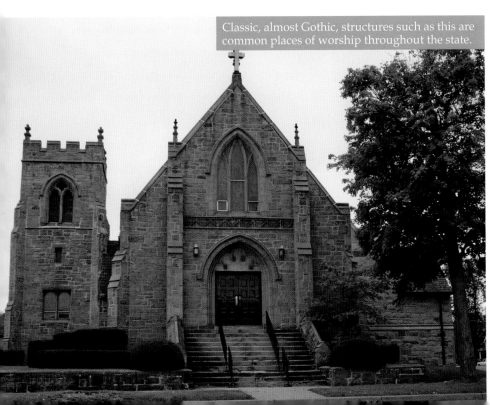

Classic, almost Gothic, structures such as this are common places of worship throughout the state.

The twin peaks of Nashville, Tennessee.

Tennessee churches host some of the most interesting graveyards dating back to the pre-Civil War era.

Memphis tells America to "Return To Christ" in a monument found just outside the city.

Tombs like this are common on religious grounds throughout the state.

This modern cemetery shares holy ground with a Civil War soldier cemetery only a few feet away.

The Christ Museum and Gardens is a holy place found in Gatlinburg, Tennessee, where believers can see floral displays and tableaus set up representing multiple stories from the Bible.

Indian Temple, Belle Meade, Tennessee.

Closing

I hope you have enjoyed this brief pictorial tour through some of my favorite areas of Tennessee. It's a beautiful state filled with history, culture, and loads of wonderful people. There is definitely something for everyone and new sights to discover every day.

Bibliography

Beck, Ken. *Terrific Tennessee.* Premium Press America, 1996.

Bergeron, Paul. *Tennesseans & Their History.* University of Tennessee Press, 1999.

Calloway, Brenda. *America's First Western Frontier: East Tennessee – A Story of the Early Settlers and Indians of East Tennessee.* Overmountain Press, 1989.

Cottrell, Steve. *Civil War in Tennessee.* Pelican Publishing, 2001.

Crutchfield, Jennifer. *Chattanooga Landmarks: Exploring the History of the Scenic City.* The History Press, 2010.

Ewing, James. *A Treasury of Tennessee Tales.* Thomas Nelson, 1997.

Finger, John. *Tennessee Frontiers.* Indiana University Press, 2001.

Guy, Joe. *The Hidden History of East Tennessee.* The History Press, 2008.

Hargrove, Erwin. *Prisoners of Myth: The Leadership of the Tennessee Valley Authority.* University of Tennessee Press, 2001.

Harkins, John. *Metropolis of the American Nile: A History of Memphis & Shelby County, Tennessee.* Guild Bindery Press, 1995.

Hollis, Tim. *See Rock City: The History of Rock City Gardens.* The History Press, 2009.

Hoobler, James. *A Guide to Historic Nashville, Tennessee.* The History Press, 2008.

Kerr, Les. *Tennessee.* Graphic Arts Books, 2004.

Lacey, Theresa. *Amazing Tennessee.* Rutledge Hill Press, 2000.

Leiter, Kelly. *The Tennessee Valley.* University Press of Kentucky, 1998.

Lovett, Bobby. *The Civil Rights Movement in Tennessee.* University of Tennessee Press, 2005.

Luna, Kristin. *Tennessee Curiosities*. Globe Pequot, 2010.

Manley, Roger. *Weird Tennessee.* Sterling, 2011.

Olwell, Russell. *At Work in the Atomic City: A Labor and Social History of Oak Ridge, Tennessee.* University of Tennessee Press, 2008.

Schatz, Bob. *Tennessee: Simply Beautiful.* Farcountry Press, 2005.

Weeks, Terry. *A History of Tennessee.* Clairmont Press, Inc., 1989.

West, Carroll. *Tennessee Encyclopedia of History & Culture.* Rutledge Hill Press, 1998.

Woodworth, Steven. *Six Armies in Tennessee.* Bison Books, 1999.